A CAST OF

POETRY BY PHILIP GROSS

ART BY JOHN EAVES & F J KENNEDY

ISBN 0 9514076 4 3   A Cast of Stones (pbk)

Designed & Produced by Stephen Nelson.

Printed by Barwell Colour Print, Midsomer Norton,
and bound by W H Ware & Sons, Clevedon.

First published 1996 by Digging Deeper,
4 Green Street, Avebury, Marlborough, Wiltshire SN8 1RE.

accept an invitation to come back and study them in depth, because the poems - poems more about the idea of the pictures than the things themselves, and more about the idea of Stonehenge than the actual stones - were already on their way.

Stonehenge is a tangible fact. But human beings need meanings, and in the face of the stones' stout refusal to let themselves be decoded every age has come up with theories and stories… which of course say more about us, in our time and our place, than they say about the stones. A glimpse of John's drawings, too quick to "read" them consciously, still imprinted me with something of the mass and form, but particularly of the near-abstract elusiveness of the shapes. The trilithons were already becoming doorways, secret openings, empty proscenium arches, children's games.

All of this might still have been poems-about-paintings if it had not been for the music. I was already performing poems with John's free-form improvising outfit, Vanilla Allsorts; the Henge poems were written in the spirit of that music, for the group to build on. I had written words for songs before, but this collaboration was equal, side by side. Music was

Secret Openings: Collaborating On
A Cast Of Stones

I am a writer - a poet, novelist and playwright - but I know what words can't do. When I see a visual artist thinking in colour and shape, or hear a musician thinking aloud in pure sound, I am filled with envy and pure curiosity. Once I walked with a painter friend in a Cornish wood and she remarked casually, "Aren't the daffodil leaves blue today?" *Blue?* I realised with a dull jolt that I'd been walking in the same wood and seeing less than she saw; I was walking in a painting-by-numbers landscape crudely labelled with words like "leaf" and "green". So when I came to work with F.J. Kennedy on Avebury and John Eaves on Stonehenge I wondered: what did I, a writer, have to give them in return?

We knew what we did not want. Not poems with illustrations, and not poems-about-paintings either, though both things are genres in themselves. (If you have read U.A. Fanthorpe's poem *Not My Best Side* you can never look at Uccello's *St. George And The Dragon* in quite the same way again.) True, John's drawings of Stonehenge existed before my poems. I saw them once, stacked in his attic, but I did not also a neutral language, neither words nor image, between John's pictures and me. Lacking the language of art, I could hear his charcoal rendering of the trilithons as music, and the poems proposed rhythms of their own to counterpoint them, dancing in their shade. Once the doors started opening, they interconnected endlessly - into visual image, personal memory, myth or archæology.

The collaboration with F.J. was different. We were brought together by Mike Pitts, archæologist, photographer, restaurateur and godfather of *A Cast Of Stones*. In place of John's stark but shifting monochrome, I was looking at F.J.'s fields of rich colour crowding in from sky, hills, vegetation… almost wilfully *not* giving the great stones pride of place.

We talked, cautiously. We walked among the stones, not unfriendly but not yet friends. She was wearing dark glasses in the bright sunlight; seeing the place reflected in those lenses made me wonder again: how can I know what those eyes see? Did they see colour, form and movement, while I looked at the same stone and saw… what? I had come intending to write images in haiku style - something crisp, clear and visual. In fact I came intending to write as much like a visual artist as I could. What followed showed me how wrong I could be.

The trigger was nothing you could quite call real. It was a photograph, in the museum, of a skeleton. Even the bones do not exist; they were destroyed in the Blitz, having been moved to London for safe keeping. That sort of irony attached itself to them quite naturally. They had been found beneath a fallen megalith, not a Bronze Age burial but a mediæval spectator, probably, caught when the stone was toppled circa 1320. A little pouch of tools identified him as a barber-surgeon. A doctor, I thought… until I turned to a respectable history of medicine. Barber-surgeons were dismissed in one page: "usually uneducated and incompetent", they "often doubled as barbers, pedlars, tinkers, conjurors and ratcatchers". And there was his grin, looking at me sidelong, waiting for his story to be told.

Story, narrative. Metaphor, hints, implications. Those were the writerly things I had been seeing while my artist-collaborators saw colour, pattern, mass and form. I gave up trying to write a painting and slipped into the first draft of a sequence of poems that became a story, historical romance almost, of love, adultery, jealousy and death. The notebook observations that might have been haiku, an accurate record of Saturday 4th September 1993, were still there, but it was the barber-surgeon who was seeing them, wry and rather yearning, finding echoes of his own tale littered round the place. Looking at F.J.'s paintings again with his eyes, I saw that their bright flat surfaces were actually full of sensual curves and secret openings. Knowing the barber-surgeon by that stage I thought: well, he would, wouldn't he? Somehow, separately, the poems and the paintings had touched something in common. As far as I know, the barber-surgeon's narrative is all lies (though I feel they are the kind of lies he might have spun himself). Yet it was, it is, in some sense, really there.

If I had been there with a different painter, on a different day, would it still have been there, or something else entirely? The Stonehenge experience was different again. This book is the record of two sets of doors that opened unexpectedly. Step inside…

Philip Gross

A version of this article first appeared in Modern Painters, Winter 1995.

A Game Of Henge

1.

A game of Henge, my masters?
The pieces are set. We lost the box
with the instructions years ago.

Do you see Hangman? Or
Clock Patience? Building bricks
the gods grew out of? Dominoes?

It's your move. You're in the ring
of the hills, of the stones, of the walls
of your skull. You want to go?

You want out? Good - that's
the game. Whichever way you turn
are doors. Choose. Step through, so...

And whichever world you stumble into
will be different from all the others, only
what *they* might have been,
                                   you'll never know.

2.

Those stony backs. A scrum around a whisper:
    Hush. Hiss. Who?
Why won't they let you in? No, it's a
      secret secret
      won't tell YOU...

A playground wide as Wessex. Wire barbs
    the wind whines through.
You'd wait a hundred years and couldn't ask.
      It's *secret secret*
      won't tell YOU.

Don't dare. You dare yourself to dare
    and then you do.
They turn and... What's the game? *You* are.
    And it's *Sticks And Stones*
    and you're on your own
        and it's Piggy In The Middle
        and the piggy is YOU.

3.

Once upon a time a small
stone viaduct got bored
with going somewhere. So it curled
up snug, forgetting all
about timetables and connections.
Now its train of thought runs round
and round forever and
its little whistle goes
      who who

     who who

    who who

4.

It wasn't so much the stones
I loved, aged nine.
It was the word *archæology.*

That and finicky diagrams
showing circles complete
with the things that weren't there:

post holes, lost stones…
like the scene of the crime,
the victim's parting gesture

plotted on the pavement,
or the files the dentist kept on me
and everyone, living and dead

cheek by jowl in his metal safe.
Like the shudder and thrill
when I read in the paper:

they identified him by his teeth.

5.

The chips are down,
cast runestones,
ruins of a meaning
lying as they fall,

closed books
in crusty bindings,
picture frames
that frame blank wall.

We read the stones
to tell our fortunes.
They say
bugger all.

6.

We're back to back
in a circle of stones

like a stopped clock,
gap-toothed cogs,

and whatever's the time
we can't tell any more

than the face knows what it's showing.
If the sky can see

what figure our two bodies
make together it's not letting on.

I don't want to turn, to feel
one more click of the ratchet.

If we could hold perfectly still…
But the sun

and stars and other working parts
work on. A grain of quartz

winks with its perfect timing.
We can't see the shadows move;

they do, and will touch one
of us before the other

no matter how close
we huddle, equally afraid

it might be me,
it might be you.

7.

The image won't come clear.
My windscreen slurries.
Wipers whinge and smear
beating down an always-

rising surf of sleet.
Out of the blaze
of some fool's undipped headlights
something sways

to its feet towards me, thrown
into my path, huge
as a henge of drunken stones.
I swerve and slew

to a shudder and it's gone,
just the shadow of the crash-kerb, while
with only the hard shoulder to cry on,
I do, don't know why.

I've killed the lights
and watched the wipers judder to a hush.
The screen smatters white
then darkens slowly as a crust

of silence seals me in
like a troll caught out at dawn alone,
like no-fool-like-an-old-fool Merlin
who built henges and was locked in stone.

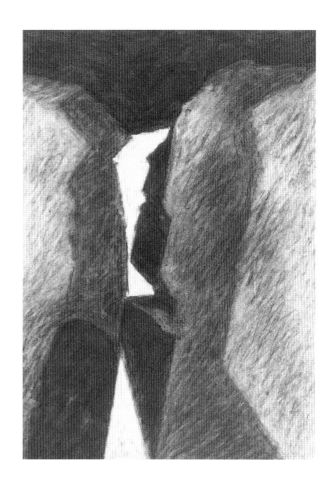

8.

These are the stones.

These are the stones
that hold the ground
nobody owns.

These are the stones
that hold the ground
of doubts and dreams
nobody owns.

These are the stones,
the dancing floor
of doubts and dreams
that hold the ground
nobody owns.

These are the stones
nobody owns,
that hold the ground
of doubts and dreams.
Who can control
the dancing floor?

These are the stones
of doubts and dreams
of peace, it seems,
that hold the ground
who can control?
Nobody owns
the dancing floor.

These are the stones
that hold the ground,
the dawn patrol
of peace, it seems.
Who can control
the dancing floor
of doubts and dreams
nobody owns?

These are the stones
nobody owns,
the dawn patrol
who can control
the dancing floor
of doubts and dreams
of peace, it seems,
that hold the ground
set out of bounds.

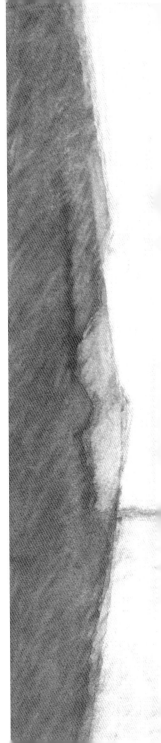

A knock at the door:
the dawn patrol!
Who can control
the dancing floor
of peace it seems
nobody owns.
These are the stones
that hold the ground
of doubts and dreams
set out of bounds.

     …stones
    …dancing
…doubts and
     …peace it seems
  nobody owns
     …no
a knock at the door
a knock at the door.

These are the stones.

9.

They've left their imprints in the rain
even larger than they were
as if the stones

had been whistled off, called home
to lie down with their masters
and there's only

their shadows left standing, hugely
patient but shuffling slightly
- or is it just

gusts and flurries of rain? They shift
from foot to foot like the queue
for the very last bus.

10.

Now you see them… Now you don't.
    The more you think you see, the more you stare.
    The more the shutter clicks, the less they're there.
        The final trick!

We'll need several thousand volunteers.
A million tons of concrete.

Cast a bald and bare
sarcophagus and seal them deep,

safe as nuclear waste.
Let there be steps like an Aztec pyramid

and on the top a pyre
to which processions of the unemployed

will bring every photograph and postcard,
all the evidence. A tourist guide or two

will be sacrificed (with simultaneous translation).
It will be dreadful. It will be taboo.

Then let the rumours begin. A hint. A joke
in poor taste. Let there be dubious

old men at dusk nudging over the mound
with their hazel twigs twitching. And in bus-

shelters and bike sheds let young whispers start.
The true Stonehenge will rise

again, story by story, faithfully
restored in all its glory:
        whopping lies.

A Day At The Earth-house

"Underneath one particular stone in the south-west quadrant were not only mediæval pottery shards but the crushed skeleton of a barber-surgeon, complete with leather purse containing scissors, probe and money."
The Avebury Monuments: DOE Handbook

Mediæval surgeons "often doubled as barbers, pedlars, tinkers, conjurors and ratcatchers."
The Study of Medicine, Vernon Coleman

1. Under The Stone

Dry bones.
Here's enough for a finger
to crook, to poke. Or two.
Diggers, down on your knees
like a priest's flock to a relic

or a wife who tries to gather every
fragment of the crock
her man flung at the wall
as if she might piece
their lives together.

Can these bones live?
Dust them, toothbrush them free
as if the lie of them
held all the clues: whose hand
might drop its pouch of tools

and throw itself open
like cards slapped down
    (dry
    bones, my bones)
the devil take it, win or lose.

2. Earthwork

   Like a splash
in a green pond baized with duckweed
that a child could run onto
      and drown

      ditch and bank
spread; trees, stones, houses
bob in the jolt of a shockwave
      like visible sound

      where it sank,
whatever, pitched in. Still the ripples
spread till you can't tell them from
      encircling downs.

3. An Old Story

   A boy, hung back
from a pother of family picnic,
      squares up to a stone -

come on, let's be having you.
   Blank as his dad's
face after work, set in its creases,

      it won't rise for play-
fights he can win. Diminished
      he stumps after mum.

4. Long Barrow

Up the hill in the tump
they banked their bones
like family silver
to be brought out on high holidays.

Quite a picnic: *hey
kids, we're going to tea
with great-great-grandad.
Leave the dog at home.*
                              Oh,

      but to be introduced
      to the bloodline, the many-
      branching trickle-down of it,
      your juices

      still quick in their skin… Now
      wouldn't that be something
      when your bones are dry
      like mine?

5. Unbecoming

Because it's there
and has curious
crannies and holds,
though she's nearly
too old for this,
skirt bloomered up,
the girl climbs,

slips and
for a moment hangs,
arms straight, feet
frisking, sleeked
as if this was her best
dive ever, ripping under-
water like a bridal veil.

6. On The Cusp

If I could leave it alone, after so
    many late-September Saturdays…
        If I didn't have to feel
            the still-tender spot,
                the soon-to-cool not-long-begun

time on the cusp, with lovers
    on the south slope
        of the earthwork, side
            by side, half-turned
                to each other, two-in-one

like the wings of a butterfly,
    tattered Red Admiral
        edging and angling, not
            to lose one blink
                of what's left of the sun.

7. On First Seeing Silbury Hill

The long she of the downs
       (Compared to her the great flasher of Cerne
       and all that white-horse sky-gymkhana are the chalk
       scrawls of a pavement artist before rain…)

stirs in her sleep
or pretends for you, flexing so

the slope from hip to waist
or collarbone to nipple tip

is silk pegged in the wind,
skin alert to be touched, like an ache

because only your eye
can stroke it. And the way

she seems to shift
as you walk deeper, opening a green

cleave in the snug of it,
a glimpse of this soft nub, lipped

in ground that sometimes
in a season darkens

to marsh, responding
to the mood swings of the moon.

8. Habitation

An old ewe shared with me the shade
of a stone that she'd rubbed to a high
dim gloss like the face in the Shroud.
I broke my bread; she watched, one eye

blue-blind like a cloud past the moon,
the other a keyhole, a crack
of indoor dark. What did it mean,
the way the village turned its back

on the circle that even the church
would not enter? I could almost see
how it begged to be rubbed, that old itch
folk just can't leave be.

9. One From The Tarot Pack

Beneath an overhanging stone he squints up,
a guide book dangling from his hand,
while she stands off a little, eager still

to be impressed. His head's on one side,
neck cricked back, for all the world
(she starts as if she's seen) the Hanged Man.

10. Cold Calling

    Always the same, stepping in
to that suddenly-everything-happening
    stopped. The same dumb
fish mouths. The children one by one
    then mothers, wardful, then
trundling doubts into place, the men.
    A cleared space where the show
begins again. And most times stones
    seem more likely to yield
than these dull faces. But I start my spiel.

Nominy dominy nihil abominy...
Latin, good as the priest's. Someone give me a stone,
which hand's it in? There, gone! And here's one
for the kiddies, little game called Knucklebones...

(She
in the doorway,
a child or two loose at her knee,
hair pale as unreaped wheat, oh the first
rain could grey it. Her eyes quickened, levelling with me.)

Goodfolk, moisten my throat
and I'll sing you the news
from the courts of high France
from the land of the Jews...

(He,
hand laid
on her waist, no
question but a heavy
husband's hand: *What sort of man
are you, stranger? And what can you do?*)

I twirled my little scissors, caught the sunlight, flash and clack.

*A barber-surgeon at your service,
sir. Might catch a rat
for you. Or let a little blood.
Or trim your thatch.*

    All grinned, but him.
Some stoat's-piss cider passed round,
    taking the heat from the day.
And she, waiting on everyone, waiting
    on him. And for me.

(Blunt blade itching for her stone.
Should have let some blood. My own.)

11.   Sarsens

Heathen knights, felled
full length in their armour,
face down on the hillside, still
they dream us harm.

Will's girl, out late,
let just the shadow of one
touch her ankle and the child she got
was born cold as a stone.

We say: Bury them.

When a good man loses wife or cow
or strength the stones know why and how.

We say: Bury them, bury them.

Don't breathe a word of them after
but be careful where you dig or plough.

12. Hallowed Ground

On entering from the south-west by the car park
    observe in the field
to your left these geometric chalk-etched figures
    cognate in their symmetry
less to white horses than corn circles.

    Note too at the east
and west extremities (a solar orientation?)
    pairs of post-holes, empty,
which suggest poles may have been removed
    to be replanted annually
for a seasonal ritual. (Just when you think
    you've got the story
straight somebody always moves the goalposts.)

13. Deposits

Late sleepers in the earth-house,
the long bunker on the hill,

this can't be *you*, this depart-
ment store of bones, thighs racked

by size, this lego-set of vertebrae,
toe bone winked in an eye socket. No,

whatever was you has leached out
with your private juices, out and down

into stream into soil into grass into cow
into milk and into children's bones again

and of your finest feelings all we know
is that you ached. Arthritis. Ask the bones.

14.   Family Features

Our patch our stream our ditch and bank
our compass our burial mounds
our birthmarks on a close horizon
our naming our limits our bounds.
       Our toast: us and ours!

(A door ajar, a glimpse of her
and him, leaning closer to touch
one candle to another, held
till the light swells:
            them and theirs.)

Our chips off the old stone our tilt
of the nose our ways of handing down
old scars old scores in the weary old
bone our kids our common ground.
       Our toast: us and ours!

(Their dusk, their squealing in the eaves,
martins sip-tilting home, framed so
for someone in the dark... Then she
looks up, no longer
            unawares.)

15. Rites

In the church of St James, at his post
on the font a priest with no face holds two smooth-

coiled snakes at bay. The two stone avenues
coil up over the hill to the henge. Out of sight

the organ tunes up for a wedding and, white
ribbons shivering, a sit-up-and-beg

white Morris takes a road marked red
on the map, that cuts the henge. A sideways

glance: the bride in the back looks, let's say
carsick, as they slow to thread between

great stones. The dancers on the green
wag their hankies like aunts on the end

of the platform of centuries: Morris men
in white laundered blouses slashed -

cross their hearts - with these sashes
of blood red, like barber's poles.

16. Clearings

Raw monks in a row
on a rough wooden bench.
They bow their heads to me.

Don't I work to the good
Brother Abbot, hacking
clearings in the growth

that ramps around
your lawful habitations,
home to who knows, to those

without station or hope
of salvation? Sans haircuts
any man among us might run wild.

Then again, sun beats
the pale shaved spot.
Too much blood in them,

it heats, the Abbot mutters.
Lest the pot come to the boil
let them be bled.

17. A Nice Line In Blood

Two pints of monks' blood. A goodly black pudding
that would make. And holy, too.
Fully half a yard long. I'll show it as a relic,
St Valentine's… big toe, parson, to you.

Never fails with the women, that one. So
why do I lose the thrust now, as her eye
catches mine? As if the stones
had taken one step closer, narrowing the sky.

18. Vespers

My husband is a good man
a sound a straight a strong and
many's the woman would be glad and so I am

but

my husband is a good man a
sound a straight a strong.… And
around and again, dare not stop.

Like plainchant to my ears, this
litany. My Vespers.
Let me listen all night long.

19. Lay

As I passed through
    the Holy Land
time lay scattered
    on the sand

broken columns
    shards of Rome
earth won't take
    her children home

(*You were never in the Holy Land,* she said, sharp. Then that glance
turned, the flat of the blade, and she was laughing. *No more talk.*
Sing on.)

England mulches
    under rain
dykes fill banks seep
    mud again

hush-child-hushing
    false and true
        secrets stones
          bog oak and bones
I would not have them
    bury you

(*Is that all, then?* she teased, stretching back on the stone.

It was. He saw us.)

20. Dating

Purple gobbets on the sarsen.
Birdshit dates us: elderberry season.
    At the burial site
ants' wings found in the lowest stratum
nail the death on August. Last
    month's mating flight.

21. Stone Burial

The men had ropes around the stone
like a cornered beast. There was a pit prepared,
a heave-ho bellow:
    One… two… three! But no,

the stone's the Devil and won't budge
and every able-bodied Christian man must…
You too, stranger. Yes, you!

Here I go
where her good man beckons
into the cleared space. The shadow of the stone.
Brace yourself there. One… two…
thr…

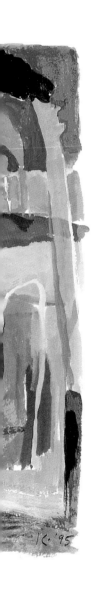

22.   Crack

I know my bones. Which snapped. Pain? No,
I was a blade of lightning snickersnacked

lifting her face from the dark of her life
and all the generations in the earth-house stacked

like turves, brief flares of wives and daughters
interlaid with men. As I turned, in the crack

of the stone door a cat couldn't tease through,
I stuck. Wanting out. Wanting back.

23.   Improvements, Circa 1700

The burning-pit blackens.
Straw packed to a mattress
flares as a stone falls.
Flounced-up ash folds back

like an old superstition.
What resemblance to Hell
once was grows hazy.
Stone whickers with heat.

A *pshaw!* of steam
as cold water is poured.
Crack. Then sledgehammers
set to. Men build walls.

24. Resurrection

And last the archæologists, the resurrection men,
pose with their big-game bag: a stone
trussed, tractored, block-and-tackled up,

a great slave at an auction, hung with chains.
And in the pit? A sidelong flattened grin. Dry bones.
Facts? Male,

only moderate height. Slight build. Neck
fractured in several places. Artefacts?
Pouch, leather, with

metal probe, scissors, 3 coins
(dated circa 1300, one of them French),
some shards of pot nearby.

Scarcely a *Christian* burial.

25. The Barber Surgeon's Song

Here's one for my probe,
my prick of wit
to get under the skin,
my goad, my God,
what pouches have I
kept it in?

Here's two for my scissor-
legs' well oiled hinge
opening time and again
to cut through thou-shalt-knots,
too sharp I hope
to cause much pain.

Here's three for the coins
from here and there
I never did spend.
Two even, one odd.
The reckoning. That's
it. The end.

26. Squaring The Circle

As right-angled chocks
off a pot-belly stone
are mortared back in place,

as ex marks the spot,

as cart tracks grown
to highways cut the cake
of the henge so a car

like a child's chalk drawing,
pretty lady in the back,
can putter through,

as a circumcising groove
makes a prick-tip monolith
a holy cross,

as square pegs hammered
pinch in holes,
we'll square the circle yet,

as the bowl of the sky
is cracked by vapour trails today
and however we try

to stick the bits together
there'll always be one we can't find
so it won't hold water.

That's what lets in time and rain.

Digging Deeper